When Mourning Breaks
Coping with Miscarriage

MELISSA SEXSON HANSON

MOREHOUSE PUBLISHING

Morehouse Publishing
P.O. Box 1321
Harrisburg, PA 17105

Morehouse Publishing is a division of the Morehouse Group.

Printed in the United States of America

Cover design by Trude Brummer

Library of Congress Cataloging-In-Publication Data

Hanson, Melissa Sexson.
 When mourning breaks : coping with miscarriage / Melissa Sexson Hanson.
  p. cm.
 Includes bibliographical references.
 ISBN 0–8192–1757–3 (pbk.)
  1. Miscarriage—Religious aspects—Christianity—Prayer-books and devotions—English. I. Title
 BV4907.H345 1998
 242'.4—dc21

                                                                            98-26074
                                                                              CIP

*This book is lovingly dedicated
to my second child, whom I lost at six weeks.
May the bud of your life inspire mourning hearts
to break forth as blossoms of God's healing love.*

CONTENTS

PREFACE

The morning that I lost my baby will forever be etched in my mind. In just moments I went from the innocent bliss of motherhood to the dreadful shock of miscarriage. I never dreamed that this nightmare would happen to me, especially since my pregnancy had been such a miracle. The simple question "Why, God?" blackened my soul and shook the very foundation of my life, leaving me full of anger and despair. All my precious plans lay shattered at my feet. Worse yet, my relationship with God seemed broken beyond repair. The emotional pain of having such an intricate part of my being ripped from my heart plummeted me into a terrible state of confusion. Not only did I dismiss any hope of God rebuilding my dreams, but I also even began to doubt that the Lord existed.

What happened during the next few months, however, changed my life for eternity. As a result of God's renovating power, I now possess a fervent desire to share my experiences with others suffering from the devastation of miscarriage. This collection of short devotional thoughts contains nuggets of scripture illustrated through true personal experiences. Each one builds on the other, taking the reader step-by-step through the grieving process of denial, anger, blame, depression, acceptance, and restoration. The following meditations offer both refreshing insights into God's passionate desire for an intimate relationship with the brokenhearted and practical examples of the amazing peace of God's abiding presence in the soul.

I guess I never really understood what the Bible meant when it said that "joy comes in the morning" (Psalm 30:5, NKJV) until I lost my children through miscarriage. Now I believe that this text not only refers to that glorious Resurrection day, when I will be reunited with my little ones, but it also is a promise for today, describing the wonderful gift God offers to all during their darkest hour of grief. Just as the sun banishes the blackness of night, so God's infinite love shines the brightest—when mourning breaks.

A Gift from God

Take delight in the Lord, and he will give you the desires of your heart.
Commit your way to the Lord, trust in him, and he will act.
                                        Psalm 37:4–5 (NRSV)

I'm pregnant." The very words made my heart skip a beat as I stared at the two pink lines of the home pregnancy kit, half afraid that one might disappear. This morning, after more than three years of trying to have children and taking numerous infertility drugs, the impossible had finally happened, and I was overjoyed. I couldn't wait to tell my husband that our prayers had been answered. But first I had to be sure that it wasn't a mistake. Immediately, I drove to the doctor's clinic for a blood test, all the while pleading with God for a miracle.

When I arrived at the lab a few minutes later, the technician drew my blood and promised to call with the test results sometime that afternoon. Slowly the hours dragged by, but at last I heard the phone ring. With trembling hands and a fluttering heart, I picked up the receiver. On the other end, I heard the nurse ask, "How would a September baby sound to you?"

Unable to believe her words, I stammered back, "Does that mean I'm pregnant?"

"Yes. Congratulations."

Moments later, after scheduling my first maternity visit, I hung up the phone and ran to find my husband. In a voice full of emotion, I choked, "Honey, you're a father." As the impact of my words filtered through his surprise, he took me in his arms and squeezed me tightly. We had never been happier.

Mercifully shielded from the devastation that lay ahead, we rejoiced in this precious gift of life. Perhaps the miracle of my pregnancy would later become a cushion for the traumatic events looming ahead in our future. But for the time being, we joyfully praised God for giving us the precious fulfillment of our hearts' desire.

Answered prayers are gifts of God's gracious love.

Miracles of the Past

Trust in the LORD with all your heart, and do not rely on your own insight.
In all your ways acknowledge him, and he will make straight your paths.
                                                        Proverbs 3:5–6 (NRSV)

A s I look back over my life, I realize that God worked many miracles so that
I would be physically able to have children. This evidence of the Lord's love
would later give me strength when I needed it most.

The first miracle took place when I was eight months old. My mother almost
fainted when the doctor told her that one of my ovaries had slipped through an
opening in my abdominal wall, causing a lump the size of an egg. Immediately,
I was rushed into surgery for a strangled hernia. The specialist had to retrieve the
ovary and repair the hole. Amazingly, a portion of this ovary would be the only
one remaining after my second emergency surgery.

This time I was sixteen and had taken my brother into the doctor for a check-
up. During the visit I happened to mention that I was having some occasional
pain in my abdomen. Reassuring me that it was probably only cramps, the doctor examined me. To his horror, he discovered a lump in my abdomen the size
of a grapefruit. He immediately ordered a sonogram and found a rare kind of

tumor encompassing both of my ovaries. Because of its rapid growth, the doctor was almost certain it was cancerous. I can remember wondering as a teenager whether or not I'd ever have the chance to get married or have a baby. Perhaps I didn't have that long to live!

Miraculously, the tumor was benign. The first question that I asked after I awoke from my operation was, "Will I be able to have children?" The surgeon replied that it was still possible, although no one could be certain. He had been forced to remove all but a small portion of one ovary. Hopefully, that tiny piece would continue producing eggs. I thanked God profusely for this tiny piece of hope.

Pregnant, now all those prayers seemed to be materializing before my eyes as my appetite grew, along with the new life developing in my womb. I wanted everyone to know about the miracle pregnancy that the Lord had so graciously granted. Never before had my confidence in God been stronger.

Lord, I praise you for the miraculous way you have led me in the past. Help me to rely on your faithfulness for the future.

Not One Heartbeat of Hope

LORD, when we are with you, we are like a woman giving birth to a baby; she cries and has pain... We gave birth, but only to wind... Your people have died, but they will live again; their bodies will rise from death.
Isaiah 26:17–19 (NCV, emphasis added)

I can't ever remember feeling better than I do right now, I thought contentedly as I sat in the waiting room of the clinic, happily flipping through baby magazines. I was three months into my first pregnancy, and I couldn't wait to hear my child's heartbeat for the first time. My husband had taken the day off from work for this joyous occasion, and both of us could hardly contain our excitement as we waited for the nurse to call our name. Inside, I carried on a silent conversation with my unborn baby. *I can't wait to hold you, little one. It seems like all my life I've wanted to be a mother. You are such a miracle! We have waited for you for so long. All those infertility treatments must have worked, or maybe God just decided that it was time. I don't know. I'm just thankful to finally have you. I love you so much already!*

A nurse interrupted my thoughts as she called our name and ushered us into an examination room, telling me to lie down on the table. I felt a jellylike substance on my abdomen, and then a cold metal instrument touched my skin. Suddenly,

I heard a rhythmic sound, similar to ocean waves crashing on the shore. Grinning confidently, I turned to the nurse and exclaimed, "That's it, isn't it? I can hear our baby!" My delight bubbled out with every word.

Before the nurse could respond, the worried expression on her face sent a sudden chill to my soul. "Unfortunately what you're hearing is your own heartbeat, not the baby's. I'm having a little trouble locating it, but I'm sure the doctor won't have any problem." She tried to sound confident.

Before I could fully grasp the implication of her words, the nurse disappeared, and the doctor took her place. The procedure was repeated, and once again, no heartbeat was found. What had been joyful anticipation instantly turned into foreboding fear. In desperation, I glanced at my husband for reassurance, only to find his expression similar to my own. The sonogram confirmed the awful truth—our baby was dead.

In a state of shock, I left the clinic with tears of unbelief streaming down my cheeks. *This can't be happening. Only moments ago, I was so happy. Oh Lord, please wake me from this terrible nightmare!*

I knew that God would hear me. I just didn't realize how much time would pass before my prayer would be granted.

God's simplest answers are far greater than life's hardest questions.

All Out of Miracles?

Give ear to my words, O LORD; give heed to my sighing. Listen to the sound of my cry, my King and my God, for to you I pray. O LORD, in the morning you hear my voice; in the morning I plead my case to you, and watch.

Psalm 5:1–3 (NRSV)

Although I never saw one drop of blood or felt any telltale cramping, my body was in the process of miscarrying. Somehow I could not accept the fact that my "miracle pregnancy" was ending without even the slightest warning.

The doctor, however, did not share my doubts. In a detached, unemotional voice, she recommended a D & C, a procedure in which my uterus would be surgically scraped out, minimizing the risk of complications. Numbly, I sat listening to her, barely comprehending her words. She spoke as though my baby was just a bunch of unnecessary tissue—something I should be relieved to get rid of. I marveled at the coldness of her words.

"Why is this happening to me, Lord?" I cried out in agony. "What did I do to deserve this?"

The receptionist wrote down the time of my surgery on a card and handed it to me. Suddenly, I realized that I had only a few short hours left with my child.

Even though it was dead, I still longed to have it close. I left the clinic in a daze, my mind paralyzed in grief.

Nothing could have prepared me for the terrible shock of miscarriage. I couldn't believe that God would allow this after all my husband and I had been through. *Why, God, would you save a piece of my ovary, then miraculously allow me to get pregnant, just so I could lose my baby?* Nothing made sense. As I struggled to hang on to the last strands of my faith, memories of miracles filtered back into my mind. God had never failed me before, but what about now?

Lord, I prayed from the depths of my heart, *I don't understand why I'm going through this tragedy. I only ask that someday you will explain it to me. In the meantime, help me survive the pain of the present.*

Open for Opportunity

My grace is sufficient for you, for my power is made perfect in weakness. So, I will boast all the more gladly of my weaknesses, so that the power of Christ may dwell in me... for whenever I am weak, then I am strong.

2 Corinthians 12:9–10 (NRSV)

After my miscarriage, a whirlwind of questions spun around in my mind. *Who am I, Lord?* My heart pleaded for an answer, but confusion seemed to be the only response to my desperate cry.

I had once been a teacher with a room full of bright-eyed children, laughing and learning together. I could remember so well the delight glistening in a student's eyes after successfully completing a difficult math problem. In my heart, I could still hear a small voice whispering in my ear, "I love you, teacher." When I was in the classroom, it was so much easier to feel needed and worthwhile.

Then suddenly everything changed. After discovering my pregnancy, I decided to give up my career in order to stay home with my baby—a small sacrifice compared with the rich rewards of motherhood. I never would have regretted this decision if I hadn't miscarried a few weeks later, leaving me with a pile of unpaid bills and no income. The financial strain was more than enough reason to become depressed, but an even greater worry tugged at my mind.

A voice seemed to whisper, "What good are you to anyone?" The words cut deeply into my soul like a two-edged razor. "If you're not a mother or a teacher, what makes you think that you are worth anything?" Somehow, I had to figure out what I was supposed to do next with my life. If it wasn't working with children, then what did God want me to do?

Lord, I'm wide open to opportunity, but I don't know which way to turn. Please reassure me with your love because I feel so insecure. Only you can bring meaning to my messed-up world. Help me rely on your strength instead of focusing on my weaknesses.

A Time Bomb of Unmet Needs

And my God will fully satisfy every need of yours according to his riches in glory in Christ Jesus.

Philippians 4:19 (NRSV)

One of my greatest needs after my miscarriage was to be held. I longed for physical strength and comfort, along with the freedom of being able to express my emotions with words or sometimes just through tears. For a while, I dreaded being alone. I was afraid of the memories that were always ready to haunt my mind. Just having someone near me brought a welcomed relief to my weary soul.

Because of this desire for companionship, I tended to smother my husband. I didn't want him to leave my sight and, as unreasonable as it sounds, I resented his absence when he was gone. It was impossible for him to hold me each time I cried, even though I wished that he could. Because this need remained unmet, I began building an invisible wall around my heart, blocking Ken out of my life. I felt like he didn't really care enough about me. If he did, he would be more understanding of my feelings. Most likely, he was entirely unaware of my dilemma because I was just as guilty of not meeting his emotional needs.

Ken's coping mechanisms were exactly the opposite of mine. Being alone, or in contact only with people who were unaware of the death of our child helped him avoid the hurt waiting for him at home. Often work provided an easy means of escape. If he could stay busy enough to keep his mind from dwelling on the past, the present wouldn't be so hard. No one at work hounded him about sharing his feelings, which was a relief, since he preferred to keep them to himself. But most of all, he didn't have to face my tears, which always brought a fresh stab of pain, and that, in and of itself, was reason enough to stay away.

Together we made up a perfect formula for disaster, much like a time bomb ready to explode. Only God's infinite mercy kept us from destroying each other and our marriage. Slowly, we discovered that Christ was the only true source of fulfillment. By surrendering our unrealistic expectations of each other to the Lord, our relationship began to flourish once again.

Lord, when I long for arms of comfort, let me find shelter in your embrace. Only you can fulfill the desires of my heart without the fear of disappointment.

Fears of Separation

Do not fear, for I am with you, do not be afraid, for I am your God; I will strengthen you, I will help you, I will uphold you with my victorious right hand.

Isaiah 41:10 (NRSV)

After my miscarriage, fear attacked my former security. Suddenly, I was aware of the possibility of losing the people that I loved. Worry about their safety hounded my heart.

For instance, because my mother had a fifty-mile drive to and from work each day, I feared she might be killed in a car accident. On many occasions the roads were slick from ice or shrouded in a layer of fog. She did have some close calls, but my imagination often ran wild. Several times I found myself calling, even in clear weather, to make certain that she had arrived home unharmed. Paranoia continually badgered me, and I longed for the past when I simply assumed that she was safe.

Not only did I fear losing a loved one through death, but I was also afraid of physical and emotional separations. I never realized how deep this concern was until I attended a women's conference without my husband. While I was away,

I dreamed that Ken wanted a divorce. Perhaps I had noticed unconsciously that since the miscarriage Ken and I had distanced ourselves from one another. Because we were each so caught up in our individual grief, it was hard to comfort and support each other. Maybe this aloofness contributed to my worry concerning the stability of our relationship. Or perhaps the guilt of not being able to bear a child for my husband still haunted me. I'm not sure.

Whatever the reason, I awoke in a cold sweat. The nightmare had been so real! I could still feel the icy glare of Ken's eyes as I pleaded with him to give our marriage a second chance. My whole world seemed to crumble under my feet as waves of panic engulfed me. *How could I ever survive losing him, too?* The thought sent chills to my fingertips, even though I knew that it was just a bad dream.

My apprehension didn't totally subside, however, until I was able to reach my husband by phone the next morning. In his own patient way, he tenderly reassured me that his love for me had not wavered. Thank God that I have such a devoted husband!

Lord, please take these uncontrollable feelings of insecurity and bury them deeply in your love. Maybe then I will be able to rest safely in your arms, free from doubt and despair. I know that with you by my side I have absolutely nothing to fear.

Guilty Even Though Innocent

Are not two sparrows sold for a penny? Yet not one of them will fall to the ground apart from your Father. So do not be afraid; you are of more value than many sparrows.

Matthew 10:29,31 (NRSV)

Guilt, I have found, is a relentless accuser. After my miscarriage I was often plagued with self-accusations of things I should or should not have done during my pregnancy. Maybe I should have eaten better or exercised more. On the other hand, perhaps I shouldn't have taken any cold medicine before I realized that I was pregnant. Could this have caused me to miscarry? Even though my actions probably had little to do with the devastating results that followed, I just couldn't shake the blame embedded deep in my soul.

This was not, however, the first time I had tried to soothe an "innocent" guilty conscience. The memory of my failed attempt to save a wounded bird is a prime example of misplaced blame. One day I discovered an injured sparrow in my front yard, and I knew its fate rested in my hands. If I didn't try to rescue it, the creature was bound to become a tasty snack to some flop-eared predator. Consequently, I became its temporary mother, and the bird was patiently given milk one drop at a time. Although I fed the little sparrow faithfully, I found it dead two days later, lying facedown in its cardboard haven. Tears welled up in my eyes. Could I have accidently killed it by handling it too much? Guilt pierced my soul as I buried the tiny creature. It was all I could do, although my heart insisted that I should have done more.

As I mourn the miscarriage of my baby, my conscience is once again pricked by the needles of regret. Only this time my loss is far greater than the life of that sparrow. Could I have somehow caused the death of my child? As accusations stabbed my mind, I cried out for the gentle touch of the "Balm of Gilead." Only God's healing love holds enough power to soothe the throbbing pain of my soul.

Lord, if you care enough to remember the sparrow's fall, surely you can grant me freedom from this terrible sting of guilt. As I surrender my regret to you, my heart soars once again on the wings of your abounding mercy.

Turning Rage into Restitution

Can a woman forget her nursing child, or show no compassion for the child of her womb? Even these may forget, yet I will not forget you. See, I have inscribed you on the palms of my hands.

Isaiah 49:15–16 (NRSV)

One wouldn't think that a simple encounter could release such a tidal wave of emotion, but I'm learning that grief appears unexpectedly and has no boundaries. Waiting in line at the social security office, I spotted the protruding stomach of a teenage girl standing in a line parallel to mine. Obviously she was in her last month of pregnancy; however, her condition was not what caught my eye. Instead, my gaze focused on the large black letters of her maternity top which boldly declared, "Shit Happens," followed by an arrow pointing to her stomach. I instantly felt my face flush and my hands clench in fury. *How could she?* I screamed silently. *It's just not fair! She has what I've always wanted, and she doesn't even want it!*

As anger surged through me, I lashed out at God. And God took it. I silently shouted and screamed about how unfair life is, and God only agreed. Then, through the raging hurricane of my emotions, came a soft tender voice that repeated the same words that once stilled a stormy Galilean sea: "Peace, be still!" (Mark 4:39, NKJV). Even though human love could forsake its own, God could never forget a child drowning in a turmoil of indignation.

Lord, I know I'm losing it. I can't think straight anymore. I feel like I'm sinking in an ocean of anger, and only you can save me. Please soothe my raging emotions with the power of your calm assurance.

Conflicts and Resolutions, Part I

Put away from you all bitterness and wrath and anger... and be kind to one another, tenderhearted, forgiving one another, as God in Christ has forgiven you.

Ephesians 4:31–32 (NRSV)

It seemed that everywhere I looked women were pregnant or had babies. Somehow, just their presence sent shivers down my spine and often left me gritting my teeth. I simply couldn't cope with the heart-wrenching memories triggered by the sight of newborns or expectant mothers.

These feelings left me in quite a predicament when my sister-in-law called, saying that she wanted my husband and me to come to Oklahoma for the delivery of her baby girl. She was having a C-section, and all the family would be there for this joyous occasion. Everyone expected our presence, and I could feel the pressure building between my husband and me when I adamantly refused to go. Unfortunately, I knew I was in a no-win situation. If I remained firm with my decision, a strain was bound to occur in our family. If I relented and went, I was certain that I would become an emotional basket case. I just couldn't take a whole weekend immersed in a new-birth celebration.

In fact, I was downright mad that I had been invited in the first place. After all, my in-laws were aware of my recent miscarriage. How could they make such an unreasonable request? The more I thought about it, the more adamant I became. My husband, however, did not realize the intensity of my feelings.

Ken put off answering for as long as possible, but finally he consented to go by himself. I was furious. Now my wrath turned against him for not understanding my pain. How could he go without me? I felt betrayed. Hadn't the loss of our baby meant anything to him?

As my heart stormed in protest, I mechanically tried to worship the next morning, but for some reason, the words blurred on the page, and I could make no sense out of them. Frustrated, I cried out to God for sympathy, but none came. Quietly, the Lord reminded me that I was making myself miserable by stubbornly hanging on to my hurt instead of surrendering it to him. The more I tried to solve my problems, the more frustrated I became. Finally, in desperation I cried out:

Lord, I just can't seem to let go of my feelings. I'm so mad at everyone, especially myself. Please somehow pick up the pieces of this mess and help me to forgive even when I don't feel like it. Please resolve my turmoil with the gentleness of your love.

Conflicts and Resolutions, Part II

Call to me and I will answer you, and will tell you great and hidden things that you have not known.

Jeremiah 33:3 (NRSV)

Celebrating the birth of a new baby had a tremendous impact on my husband's view of our miscarriage. I noticed a remarkable change in Ken after he returned from his brother's. When I asked him about the events of the weekend, he didn't have much to say. The words that finally came were ones that I would always remember.

He tenderly described the tremendous emotion that was wrapped up in the moment when he held his tiny niece for the first time. As he stared into her soft blue eyes, he could feel his own misting. A miniature fist, intricately designed, curled around his little finger, squeezing it ever so gently. She felt as soft as a cotton puff, and the callouses of his work-worn hands seemed to rub against her delicate skin like sandpaper. Deep inside, he feared that she might break as he watched her wriggling in his arms.

At that moment the reality of our child's death burned itself into his mind, leaving its mark forever in his heart. Fighting back the tears, he handed the precious bundle back to her mother, knowing that he might not ever have the chance to hold a baby of his own. It was then that he realized why I hadn't come. What was a joyous celebration for others turned out to be a heart-wrenching experience for him. No longer could he view our miscarriage only from an analytical standpoint. Too much of his heart was wrapped up in its memories. Finally, our loss was real in his eyes. What had begun as a conflict in the end drew us closer together—more than I had imagined possible.

Problems become solutions in God's mathematics of life.

Pulling the Roots of Bitterness

See to it that no one fails to obtain the grace of God; that no root of bitterness springs up and causes trouble.

Hebrews 12:15 (NRSV)

Going back to our church after my miscarriage proved to be a real challenge. I remembered getting up during one church service, with tears trickling down my cheeks, and praising God for his goodness in giving us a child. Little did I know that only a few months later I would dread facing that same congregation with the news of our loss. Somehow I felt that I had let them down. I should have prayed more or studied my Bible harder. Surely it was my fault. I wasn't certain what had gone wrong; I just felt responsible.

The service seemed to last for an eternity. Many concerned members expressed their sympathy, and I managed to hold myself together as long as I didn't look anyone in the eye. *Only a few more minutes, I promised myself, then I can collapse in my car and cry all the tears I have bottled up inside of me.* At last the benediction ended. I raced to the door, hoping that no one would notice my hasty exit. Just as I thought I had made a clean escape, someone grabbed my arm. As I whirled around, I found myself face-to-face with a friend that had gotten pregnant around the same time I had. As I stared at her maternity dress, a wave of bitterness washed over me. My mind churned in envy. This was her third child. She hadn't even wanted to get pregnant. It just wasn't fair! Why her? Why now? She was the last person I wanted to see.

While I glared at her in angry silence, I couldn't help but notice the tears glistening in her dark eyes as she told me how upset she had been upon hearing of my loss. She had tried to call, but no one had answered. (I knew this was true. I had gotten her message, but I never returned her call.) The sincerity in her voice pierced my guilty conscience, and I abruptly turned to leave. Before I could dash out the door, however, she tenderly squeezed my hand and promised to pray for me.

Maybe it was her prayers that made the difference, or maybe it was just her tears. I'm not sure. But amazingly, I left church that day one step closer to becoming whole.

The roots of bitterness choke out the heart of life.

Battered by Cruel Comfort

I tell you, on the day of judgment you will have to give an account for every careless word you utter; for by your words you will be justified, and by your words you will be condemned.

Matthew 12:36–37 (NRSV)

It's amazing how much "cruel comfort" one receives after having a miscarriage. Since most people don't know how to react, they usually ignore the subject (the safe way out), try to "fix" the problem with ready-made solutions, or give standard apologies and quickly excuse themselves. A few attempt to offer some well-meaning but often hurtful words of encouragement.

One phrase that I heard many times was, "I'm sure you'll have another baby soon." Regardless of whether this was true or not, these words seldom brought comfort. One child never replaces another. Besides, in my case, we had tried for years to get pregnant; we had gone through dozens of infertility tests and treatments, and had almost given up hope of ever having our own children. Not many people knew about our struggles, and the irony of this response cut deeply into my soul. More times than not, however, I would pull out my mask and hide my hurt. The majority of people never stopped to uncover my charade.

Another response that I grew to dread was, "I know exactly what you're going through." Usually this one was followed by a story that was totally irrelevant to the pain I was experiencing. And even if the person had gone through a miscarriage, no one can know how someone else is feeling. Each has his or her own set of circumstances. No two losses are ever the same.

The phrase I hated the worst of all, however, was, "Well, it must have been God's will. The Lord takes some and leaves others." My stomach always knotted up at the cruelty of such Christian "theology." I certainly could never serve the kind of god that would willingly kill babies to take them for himself! Instead, the Bible teaches that God's heart aches for our losses and breaks from our tears. Our pain and suffering are never the Lord's will. Such claims sadly misrepresent God's flawless character of love.

Lord, help me to forgive those who "know not what they say," and accept your peace in the place of my pain. Help me to rely on the true source of comfort and strength—one that will never let me down.

Mending a Broken Heart

I call upon you, for you will answer me, O God; incline your ear to me, hear my words. Wonderously show your steadfast love, O savior of those who seek refuge.

Psalm 17:6–7 (NRSV)

It's been several months since the loss of my child, and no one wants to talk about it anymore—no one, that is, except me. For so long, I couldn't bring up the subject without crumbling into tears. Now I'm finally strong enough to share my thoughts and feelings, but who will listen? My family, my friends, and even my husband try to sidestep the issue, as if silence could erase the pain of the past. Yet grief only grows if it's buried. Deep within I long for an attentive ear.

Perhaps this desperate need was what brought me to my knees this morning. I just wanted someone to talk to, Lord, and you've promised to listen. I can pour out my heart's sorrow to you without the fear of rejection, and as my words spill out, healing begins. Tenderly, you offer me the peace of your presence. Could it be that you've been waiting for this conversation all along?

Lord, when the pain is overwhelming, and no one else seems to care, help me give you my burdens before I'm crushed under their load. I need your strength to get me through this day. As I open up my heart to you, please hear my fragile cry and fill me with your steadfast love.

Prayers are the stitches that mend a broken soul.

Finding God in a Santa Suit

I have loved you with an everlasting love; therefore I have continued my faithfulness to you.... I will turn their mourning into joy, I will comfort them, and give them gladness for sorrow.

Jeremiah 31:3,13 (NRSV)

After losing my baby, I longed to fill the emptiness of my heart. Having been raised in a Christian family, the Bible was a natural place to turn. I began looking up texts that spoke specifically about comfort in mourning, and I discovered that many of them were found in the book of Isaiah. As I read chapter after chapter of Isaiah, I was determined to find out if I could trust the God of my childhood. Was it really true that God could bring healing to my wounded soul? The surprise that lay hidden in the Bible was remarkably similar to the one I experienced one Christmas day as a youngster.

It all began when I ran to answer the doorbell and was greeted by Santa Claus, himself. He didn't have his sleigh with him, but I was much too excited to care. Even though I had never seen him face-to-face, his bright red suit, shiny black boots, and long white beard matched the descriptions I'd always read and heard about. Without the slightest hesitation, I invited him in. Oddly, I wasn't a bit afraid of this "stranger." In fact, he didn't seem very strange at all.

As he scooped me up in his strong arms and carried me over to a rocking chair, I tugged curiously on his cotton beard. Behind all those white whiskers he seemed vaguely familiar… Perhaps it was his cologne that gave him away. Or maybe it was the way he patted my head. I'm not sure. But one thing certainly stood out in my mind: I was completely content to snuggle up against his over-stuffed tummy and tell him all of my heart's desires. I had full faith that he would meet each one. I knew that he could. That was what my Christmas stories said and, as far as I was concerned, I had more than enough reason to trust him.

I guess the Lord I found in Isaiah also fit the description of God's holy book. I had read so much in the past and heard so many stories. It was easy to identify who God was supposed to be. What shocked me, however, was the "person-ableness" of God. As promises of the Bible poured into my lap like presents, I felt like a child once again. With newfound confidence, I began to share my heart's desires with the Lord, just as I had with Santa long ago. After all, this time my faith didn't depend on a man in a red suit; it was founded in the one who had enough power to wrap up my heart with ribbons of healing love.

The wonder of God can be hidden in the most surprising places.

God's Love for the Unborn

For you created my inmost being; you knit me together in my mother's womb. I praise you because I am fearfully and wonderfully made.... My frame was not hidden from you when I was made in the secret place. When I was woven together in the depths of the earth, your eyes saw my unformed body. All the days ordained for me were written in your book before one of them came to be.

Psalm 139:13–16 (NIV)

Will God save an unborn baby? For a long time, I wondered how the Lord viewed my miscarriage. Then one day I had the opportunity to ask my pastor the one question that burned deeply in my soul: "Will I ever see my child again?"

Looking down at his feet, the young man paused, clearly reluctant to respond. Finally, he stammered, "Most likely, your baby will be as if it never were..." His words hit me in the face like a cold, wet rag. Inside my stomach revolted at the injustice of his statement, and my anger flared, ready to erupt at any moment. How could I trust a god who could ignore my child's death? Didn't the Lord care about a miscarried baby? The minister's response seemed to contradict the image of God I had discovered in Isaiah.

All I wanted was a few words of assurance, just enough to get me through my awful nightmare of reality. Surely the Bible offered some hope for a mother mourning the loss of her only child. I silently vowed to search God's word for the answers to my questions. A few days later, using a concordance, I began looking up every text in the Bible that contained the words "womb," "babe," "death," "mourning," and others that were related. Amazingly, a beautiful portrait of God's love emerged before my eyes.

In Psalm 139, for instance, God speaks of the preciousness of an unborn baby. He promises that the little one's days are recorded in a special book (verse 16). After I studied this psalm, peace settled over my heart. God did care about my baby, and I was certain that someday I would be with my child again.

Thank you, Lord, for providing in your word such powerful evidence of your love—for both me and my miscarried baby.

Broken Bones and Broken Hearts

The LORD is near to the brokenhearted, and saves the crushed in spirit.
Psalm 34:18 (NRSV)

Looking back on my life, I have to say that I've had my share of physical and emotional breaks. I can't help but feel sorry for my parents because of all the worry I caused them during my adolescence. They probably thought that I was majoring in broken bones throughout my high school years. In fact, I fell in gymnastics during my first week as a freshman and broke my right arm so badly that my folks had to drive two hours in order to get a specialist to set it. Then, at the end of my senior year, I crashed again, this time water-skiing, and hyperextended my knee. After my surgery the orthopedic specialist put my x-rays on display because he was proud of the job he had done on the youngest person in Wichita to have such a severe fracture. He had to install a metal plate in my leg and put me on crutches for six months. The next summer I had another operation to remove the plate. Poor Mom and Dad. They never complained about lifting me in and out of the bathtub, carting around all my gear, and helping me down stairways. I guess these inconveniences are a part of a parent's job description. If not, I owe them overtime.

Just as my bones were mending, my heart decided to take a turn. I can still vividly remember the tragic end to a teenage romance with the boy I had planned on marrying. He was my first love, and even now, fond memories of our times together warm my heart. When he said good-bye, I was sure my world would end. Life seemed to have lost all meaning, and I had a hard time believing that God was still in control.

Now, years later and married to the right man for me, I can see God's guidance in my life. Intellectually, I know the Lord leads in ways that are not always clear. Still, after my miscarriage I feel like the hurt teenager from the past, like the young girl whose heart was crushed. Some days I wonder if I will ever recover.

Lord, I just can't bear this agony alone. How I wish that my heart could mend as easily as my broken bones. Although I struggle today to understand your plan for my life, I am reminded of your healing in the past, and it provides hope for the future. Please help me give you the pieces of my brokenness so that one day you might make me complete again.

Turning Mud into Masterpieces

O LORD… we are the clay, and you are our potter; we are the work of your hand.

Isaiah 64:8 (NRSV)

With trembling fingers I stared at my sonogram pictures taken only a few weeks earlier. As my eyes studied the black-and-white portraits of my baby, tears blurred my vision. On the sonogram pictures, my little one looked completely normal—a perfect masterpiece of God's handiwork. What had gone wrong? If there were only some reason for my child's death, perhaps then I could make some sense out of the tragedy. Not even the doctors, however, knew why the baby's heart had stopped beating.

As waves of grief rolled over me, I cried out to the Lord in agony. *Do you care that my dreams have come crashing down all around me?* I lay sobbing in utter despair. My whole world seemed to be spinning out of control. Could God still make something beautiful out of the devastation of my life? As I waited for some type of reassurance, a memory emerged in my mind. It seemed as though God was answering my questions through the use of an ageless illustration.

I could still picture the old man dressed in homespun clothes, with mud caked under his fingernails. I probably would have missed the artist in his stooped frame had it not been for the lump of clay that he was molding. Fascinated, I watched the spinning wheel as the master magically transformed the shapeless mud into the form of a bowl. The sides rose magnificently high, and I smiled in anticipation of the finished project. Just when I was certain that the bowl was complete, the potter smashed in the sides, totalling ruining its shape. In the next moment he took the ugly collapsed dish and transformed it with a few skillful strokes into a beautiful platter that sported delicate handles where the "walls" of the bowl had been. I gasped in surprise at his finished masterpiece.

Looking back at the potter's amazing ability to sculpt something stunning from an ugly piece of mud, I am reminded of God's transforming power in my life. Although at times I can see only utter devastation, the Lord pictures the final outcome. Just like the clay in the sculptor's hand, I am being formed into God's beautiful work of art.

Lord, thank you for being the master designer of lives. Help me to trust in you as you mold and break me, shaping me into your perfect masterpiece.

God's Gift of Encouragement

Praise God, the Father of our Lord Jesus Christ! The Father is a merciful God, who always gives us comfort. He comforts us when we are in trouble, so that we can share the same comfort with others in trouble. We share in the terrible sufferings of Christ, but also in the wonderful comfort he gives.
2 Corinthians 1:3–5 (CEV)

Looking back, I realize that God did not leave me comfortless throughout my time of grief. Friends were sent to support me through this terrible trial. Although many of them didn't know the best way to encourage me, others who had been through similar circumstances knew just what to say and do.

Immediately following my miscarriage, for example, I received several cards and gifts of encouragement. Being one of the teachers in a small church school, I was particularly touched by the letter from the first and second graders that illustrated the Twenty-third Psalm. Another beautiful expression of sympathy was from a parent of one of my students. She made me a blue silk flower arrangement for my wall. I treasured her thoughtfulness in remembering me with such a special gesture of love. The gift that meant the most to me, however, was a children's book with a stuffed lamb on the cover. I was amazed that my friend had chosen one with a lamb since that had been the theme of my nursery. Through this simple present I would always remember that both God and I had lost a priceless "little lamb."

Perhaps the most thoughtful gift came from a friend who told me that the church was hosting a baby shower for one of the mothers-to-be. I cringed at the thought of attending. How would I ever be able to endure a night of preparation for someone else's baby when in my heart I was still mourning the death of my own? Taking a deep breath, I bravely tried to cover up my feelings of dread and asked if I could go in with her on a gift.

She cheerfully said that I could and then she quickly added, "I thought, however, that going to the shower might be too difficult for you. So instead, why don't I take you out to eat during that time, and we'll send our gift with someone else?"

Tears of gratitude sprung instantly to my eyes as I mumbled over and over again, "Thank you. Thank you for understanding." I was amazed at her insight, since most people presumed that I had already "recovered." As I hung up the phone, I bowed my head and prayed,

Thank you, God, for showing me your great love through the precious gift of true friends!

Climbing a Mountain of Debt, Part I

If you have faith the size of a mustard seed, you will say to this mountain, "Move from here to there," and it will move; and nothing will be impossible for you.

Matthew 17:20 (NRSV)

How are we going to pay all these medical bills? My mind reeled with worry as I stared helplessly at the stack of envelopes looming like Mount Everest before my eyes. Although I had no real experience in mountain-climbing, I was sure that it couldn't be more challenging than reaching the summit of all the unpaid bills. Why did my miscarriage have to cost so much?

First, the doctor visits had to be paid for, as well as the sonograms that had been ordered. Then the surgeon and the hospital sent bills for the expenses incurred during my surgery. The anesthesiologists were next in line, followed closely by the laboratory—more costs for medicine, blood draws, and tests of all kinds. Finally, the pathologists topped off the pile with a charge for "the study and disposal of fetal tissue."

That's when I blew my top. Not only was I snowed under with all the expenses that I had knowingly incurred, but I was also expected to dish out money so that some lab technician could dissect my baby like a poor frog in a biology class. Never! Angrily, I knocked over the mound of bills with a quick swipe of my hand and stomped out the front door into the fresh air.

Lord, I really doubt that's what you meant when you promised that I could move mountains, but without your help, I'm as powerless as a mustard seed. Please help me to have faith, even when our debt threatens to crush us under its load. I'm giving you my worry because I can't conquer it alone, and I know that with your strength nothing is impossible.

Climbing a Mountain of Debt, Part II

Now faith is being sure of what we hope for and certain of what we do not see.
Hebrews 11:1 (NIV)

The end of the month came and the bills were due. I dreaded writing out the checks since I was sure that we would not have enough in our account to cover them all. Pulling a calculator out of the drawer, I began totaling the medical expenses, as well as our other bills.

I silently prayed that somehow the Lord would provide enough money to meet our debts. As I punched in the numbers, a few positive thoughts came to my mind. For example, I had been called to substitute teach several days during the past month. Besides enjoying my time in the classroom, I was especially thankful for the opportunity to earn a little extra money. I had also talked to the accounting department at the hospital and they were willing to accept a small monthly installment toward the total of our bill. Even though the payment would not include the doctor's charges or the laboratory expenses, at least the largest debt had been divided into attainable amounts.

The odd jobs that Ken had picked up on the side were also a big help. My husband had put in some long hours in an effort to make ends meet. Even though I had missed not having him home at night or on the weekends, I had to admit that his hard work was necessary if we would have any chance of paying our bills.

Hoping against hope that these extra sources of income might be enough, I began subtracting our living expenses. When I came to the utility bills, I was shocked at how little we owed. Even though the weather had been unusually mild for this time of year, I was still surprised at the small amount of electricity we had used. The VISA bill was also lower, perhaps because of our use of coupons and the drop in gas prices.

As I punched in the last number, I stared at the figure in utter amazement. Doubting my accuracy, I refigured the total and glanced back at the balance in my checkbook. Just enough. It couldn't be possible. With a heart full of relief, I wiped tears of gratitude from my eyes. I guess I'm slowly learning that with God at my side, no mountain is too high to climb.

Lord, my faith in you is multiplying before my very eyes. I can't believe how you can supply our needs when all I can see is a mountain of debt. Thank you for not giving up on me even when I doubt. I praise you for turning the "impossibilities" into opportunities that demonstrate your great love.

A Father's Love

*Let us therefore approach the throne of grace with boldness, so that
we may receive mercy and find grace to help in our time of need.*
Hebrews 4:16 (NRSV)

For as long as I can remember, I could always rely on my dad. As a child, I used to climb up on my father's lap right before bedtime and beg him to let me stay up a little longer. He would innocently smile at my mother and protest, "A few more minutes can't hurt." Contented, I would snuggle up against his chest and usually fall fast asleep. I knew I was safe in my daddy's arms.

Dad always encouraged me, even as I grew older—whether I was right or wrong, talented or not. Each test I aced, each song I sang, each accomplishment, big or small, that I achieved, Dad cheered me on. Even when I missed the mark, I never let him down. It didn't matter *what* I did; it simply mattered *who* I was— his daughter—and that was enough.

Upon losing my baby through miscarriage, I dreaded telling him that his first and only grandchild was gone. I already knew from experience, though, how he would react. Dad wouldn't blame me for eating the wrong foods or lifting something too heavy. He wouldn't tell me that this loss was God's will and that

I just needed to trust the Lord more. No. He would simply hold out his arms and comfort me. I could fall apart. I could cry in front of him. I didn't have to hide my pain. Although his heart would be aching, he would be my strength, just as he had always been in the past.

I guess, Lord, that it's partly because of my dad's support that I can come to you unafraid. When I picture your face in my mind, I always see you as looking pleased, almost proud of me. Even now, when I feel my worst, your expression doesn't change. I see no anger or blame in your eyes, only tears. I wish I could crawl up in your lap and be held close. And you do hold me—through my father's arms. I can count on your unfailing love because, after all, I'm still your daughter, and that's still enough.

Every Hair Numbered

God even knows how many hairs are on your head. So don't be afraid. You are worth much.

Matthew 10:30–31 (NCV)

Mothering has always come naturally to me. When I was just a preschooler, I loved playing house with my dolls. I had one favorite doll with long golden curls and big brown eyes that closed when I laid her down for a nap. I especially liked to style her hair with a colorful assortment of my barrettes. Perhaps I should have been a hairdresser.

My mother, however, probably would not have agreed the day she found me sitting in my bedroom happily cutting a large chunk of hair off of each doll. When she asked what I was doing, I grinned innocently and said, "I'm making a baby book for my dollies like you made me, Mommy." Chagrined, my mother suddenly remembered that only a few days ago she had shown me my baby book, which contained a lock of my hair at birth. Instead of getting angry, she simply said that I would have to play with partially bald dolls.

At the time I really didn't care much about my dolls' lack of hair, but as I stare at the baby book I purchased for my miscarried child, my heart cringes at the sight of the missing lock of hair. Would it have been straight or curly? Black or blond? I have so many unanswered questions. Yet, I know that God knows. If the Lord loves my child enough to know the number of every potential hair on my baby's head (not to mention my own), I'm certain he understands how disappointed I am. I am quietly reminded that someday I will be able to see for myself the answers to my questions. I can only pray that that day will be soon. But until then, I am comforted by the thought that the Lord knows my baby intimately, down to the very hairs on its head, and still claims this little one as part of his family.

Lord, I long to know you as well as you know me. As we grow closer, I praise you for the value I am discovering in myself and in others.

The Option of Adoption

But when the fullness of time had come, God sent his Son… so that we might receive adoption as children. And because you are children, God has sent the Spirit of his Son into our hearts, crying, "Abba! Father!" So you are no longer a slave but a child, and if a child then also an heir, through God.

Galatians 4:4–7 (NRSV)

All of my life I have wanted a little girl just like me. Perhaps this desire stems from the fact that everyone tells me I look just like my mom. I always take these comments as compliments because my mom, besides being an attractive woman, has an inward beauty sparkling through her smile that one can't help but notice. Not only do my mom and I resemble each other in looks, but we also share many similar interests. For example, we love to shop together, and sing duets at church. Because we share such a special closeness, I naturally long for a daughter of my own.

When I discovered that I was pregnant, I was certain that my dreams would soon become reality. I could almost see my little girl's black patent shoes and white leotards peeking out from under her lacy pantaloons and ruffled pink dress. I couldn't wait to hold her on my lap and tell her about all the fun things we would do together.

With the miscarriage that dream suddenly vanished like the stars in a cloudy night sky. The emptiness of my arms deepened the black void of my heart, and not even my mother's words of comfort could ease the pain of losing my child.

As time passed and no other pregnancy occurred, my husband suggested that we consider adoption, but something inside of me rebelled at the thought. What if my adopted daughter was nothing like me? How would we ever relate? Stubbornly, I refused to take that chance, fearing the unknown.

One day, however, as I sat down for my morning worship, I stumbled across a text that seemed to be speaking to me. It said that God had claimed me as his own (Galatians 4:4–7, NRSV). Now wasn't that a risk! Perhaps I should think more about adoption. What if God had a little girl, or boy for that matter, that was waiting to become a part of my family and I refused the opportunity? Could I take that chance? I resolutely closed my Bible and humbly prayed:

Lord, if adopting a baby is in your plan for my life, help me to have the courage to love someone else's child. Thank you for taking the same risk with me.

The Difficulty of Doing Nothing

Wait for the Lord; *be strong, and let your heart take courage;*
wait for the Lord.

Psalm 27:14 (NRSV)

If some people are born patient, I am definitely not one of them. Waiting for a stoplight to turn green can seem like an eternity to me. At times I pray, "Lord, please make me more patient right *now*!" Unfortunately, these kinds of prayers seem to take a while before they're answered, and I certainly don't have time to wait around. Circumstances, however, sometimes demand a little more long-suffering than I wish to deliver.

One such day found me in the doctor's office waiting for a sonogram. I was six weeks into my second pregnancy, and because of my paranoia, the doctor kindly agreed to take a look at my baby's development earlier than usual. Ken had taken time off from work to come with me for moral support, and I nervously clung to his hand, tapping my foot to the beat of my racing heart.

As the nurse called my name, I sprung from my chair and hurriedly made my way into the examination room. I desperately prayed for mercy. By the time the doctor arrived, I felt like I had run a marathon; every nerve of my body was strained from the stress of waiting. I had long passed wanting to know the outcome of the sonogram. All I wanted to do was leave. Unfortunately, I was hooked up to a steel monster that seemed certain to swallow every ounce of my dreams. As the doctor silently deciphered the images on the screen, his face showed genuine concern. Even before he said anything, tears threatened to flow from my eyes.

"There's no heartbeat, is there, doctor?" Even as I said the words, I willed them to be false. *How could this happen to me again? I can't take it a second time! Please say there's still hope!*

Aeons passed as the doctor hesitated before responding. "No, I don't see one. The baby, however, is very early in its development. Depending on when in the month you actually conceived, the heart may still begin beating in a few days. We'll just have to wait and see. The receptionist will schedule another sonogram in a week. Then we'll know for sure."

Another week! I screamed inside. *How am I suppose to last that long without knowing if my child is dead or alive?* Numbly, I made my way out of the clinic and into the car, all the while arguing with God at the unfairness of this trial. Wasn't it bad enough that more than likely I would have another miscarriage, and now, on top of that, I would have to wait? Frustration gushed through my soul as my heart shouted, *Lord, how can you do this to me!*

In the darkness of my depression came a still, small voice, *"You can't control this one, my child. Give it to me, and I promise you the strength it will take to hang on. Just trust me."*

Sometimes the best action to take is none at all.

Winning the Battle of Worry

Do not worry about anything, but in everything by prayer and supplication with thanksgiving let your requests be made known to God. And the peace of God, which surpasses all understanding, will guard your hearts and your minds in Christ Jesus.

Phillipians 4:6–7 (NRSV)

Twenty-four long hours had passed since the doctor had told me that I would have to wait a week before I would know if my baby's heart was beating. I felt like I was losing my mind. Mechanically, I went about my daily routine, trying to concentrate on cleaning the house and doing the laundry, but to no avail. Every few minutes memories of the sonogram would barge into my head, breaking down the barriers I had attempted to build.

Worry was a constant adversary. Even though I had difficulty completing the simplest task, my body ached from overexertion. My entire being rebelled at the thought of fighting this invincible foe for another minute. Defeated and wounded, I prayed: *Lord, I can't take this any longer! I feel like my mind is a broken record. Over and over, I hear the doctor's words, No heartbeat. I can't find a heartbeat. I'll never last a week, God, if you leave me like this. I admit that there's nothing I can do, so I'm giving you my helplessness. My life is all messed up anyway. I don't want it. I just wish I could die. Then at least the pain would end... Where are you, Lord? I need you now more than ever. Please just give me your peace!*

Tears spilled down my cheeks as I desperately waited for some answer. Nothing happened. No handwriting appeared on the ceiling. No angel emerged from heaven. Just stillness. Stillness. For a moment, I almost missed the answer to my prayer because of its simplicity. Quietness settled over my soul like a warm woolen blanket on a cold wintery night.

The war was over. I was defeated—or had I won? Pondering this question, I lay down on my living room couch. For the first time that day, I was able to rest.

Life's shout is never louder than the whisper of God's peace.

Finding Peace in the Storm

Now may the Lord of peace himself give you peace at all times in all ways.
2 Thessalonians 3:16 (NRSV)

When I awoke Thursday morning, realizing that in a few hours I would know if my baby were dead or alive, mixed feelings jumbled together in my mind. It had been a long week of waiting and wondering; however, since I had given the future of my child to God, a strange sense of assurance had stayed with me. It wasn't the kind of peace that said everything would be okay. It simply gave me courage for whatever lay ahead.

Throughout the week prayer had become a necessary means of survival. Every time worry pestered me, I begged God for strength. I resolutely chose to think about something else. If I still found myself struggling, I used music as my lifesaver. As notes of praise songs drifted throughout my house, my heart was comforted. Of course, there were still times that tears flowed freely as I battled with discouragement. Yet, as I surrendered my will to God, strength for endurance poured into my soul.

I was also comforted by the fact that I was not alone in this struggle. The day before our appointment was scheduled, I noticed that my husband didn't eat breakfast. Out of curiosity, I asked him why. He told me that he had decided to fast and pray for the Lord's will to be done—no matter the cost. I couldn't help but admire his decision to trust God.

We didn't speak as we drove to the clinic for the sonogram. The nurse ushered us into the same examination room and hooked me to the monitor. This time I knew what to look for. As black-and-white images appeared on the screen, our baby emerged encased within my uterus. Nothing moved, however. No rhythmic flashes greeted my silent plea. Our baby was dead. Instinctively, I glanced up at Ken. Tears trickled down his cheeks as he stared at the lifeless form on the monitor. He knew.

By the time the doctor arrived, the monitor was shaking violently with my sobs. Ken's hand gripped mine, but I barely noticed. Too many thoughts tumbled around in my mind.

A strange mixture of emotions churned inside my heart—a terrible sorrow flooded over me, along with a small amount of relief that the uncertainty had ended. Although I was now free to mourn with my husband, grief encompassed my soul. Yet, even in the midst of such confusion, a sense of calmness flowed through my being.

When life is the darkest, God's love is a lighthouse, shining with heavenly assurance.

Living in Limbo

But as for me, I will look to the LORD, I will wait for the God of my salvation; my God will hear me… when I fall, I shall rise; when I sit in darkness, the LORD will be a light to me.

Micah 7:7–8 (NRSV)

I waited for nearly three weeks for my second miscarriage to occur. As the days slowly passed, after discovering that once again our baby had no heartbeat, my devastation mounted. Instead of giving birth to my first child on its due date, I was losing our second. The irony seemed like some kind of a cruel joke.

It was bad enough to know that my child had died, but it was even worse not knowing when the miscarriage would occur. Because we were still paying doctor bills from the first miscarriage, I was determined not to have another surgery. It was just too expensive, and I thought that maybe having a natural miscarriage might somehow prevent the chance of another one happening in the future. Even though I had seen the results of the sonogram myself, I stubbornly hung on to a shred of hope that my child was still alive, since I had had no bleeding or cramping. But a few days later, when I felt the first light contraction, I knew it was no use. I just wanted to get it over with. Day after day passed, however, and nothing happened.

When will this nightmare end? I thought to myself. *What if I'm home alone when it happens, or worse yet out in public?* I secretly hoped that my husband would be with me. Since I was not very far along, I expected the miscarriage to be much like a heavy period, but regardless of the amount of pain, I was still scared. Nothing could be worse, however, than this awful waiting. Would it ever end?

Lord, I don't know how long I can survive like this. I feel like I'm living in limbo. When all I can see is the darkness of depression, please show me a glimpse of your shadow. I know that you haven't forsaken me, even though I can't always feel your presence. Just help me get through one day at a time and remember that you are all the light I'll ever need.

In the Shadow of Death

Even though I walk through the valley of the shadow of death,
I will fear no evil, for you are with me.

Psalm 23:4 (NIV)

Through blurry eyes I struggled to read this verse, taped to my bathroom medicine cabinet. I had put it there with the hope that it might strengthen me when the time came for my miscarriage. Now, as waves of pain washed over me, I clung to these words like a life jacket amidst an ocean of agony.

It was 1:00 A.M. My husband was still asleep, unaware of my misery. Part of me longed to wake him, but because I had passed only a few small blood clots, I stubbornly waited. I wanted to be certain that the miscarriage was really happening. I never thought it would hurt this much. I had been cramping for well over three weeks, but when I awoke to the feeling of a strange tightness in my uterus and a sensation of pushing, I knew that something was different. As the minutes slowly ticked by, the pain gradually worsened. Just as one contraction would fade, another one would begin, barely giving me time to catch my breath.

Around 2:00 A.M. I gave up on being brave and called for Ken. When he realized what was happening, he seemed both relieved and worried. He anxiously stood next to me, rubbing my back and squeezing my hand. But nothing he did seemed to help. How long is this going to last? Time stood still. I was surprised and scared at how strong the contractions were growing! All I could do was concentrate on getting through the pain. I began to wonder if I would actually make it through this without going to the hospital. I could see fear and frustration glinting in my husband's eyes as he helplessly watched my suffering.

Around 4:00 A.M. I grabbed Ken's hand and screamed. A sharp contraction hit and, instead of fading away, it just kept building. I could find no relief from the constant agony. My body automatically started pushing, and I felt something literally being ripped away from inside of me. Then suddenly it was over.

I don't think I'll ever forget that moment or the storm of emotions raging inside my head. The waves of pain had vanished, yet the aching in my heart remained. Although I was glad that it was finally over, the loss of our child was almost more than I could bear.

How long, Lord, will my eyes drown in tears and my dreams lay shattered? An answer came to my heart's broken cry. God simply seemed to whisper, "My arms are here to hold you, child. We can make it through this together."

The light of God's presence dims the shadow of death.

Drowning in Tears

When you go through deep water and great trouble, I will be with you. When you go through rivers of difficulty, you will not drown. For I am the LORD your God, your Savior.

Isaiah 43:2–3 (TLB)

As I mourn the death of my baby, waves of grief wash over my soul, leaving me gasping for a breath of assurance. I long to feel God's mighty hand, reaching down into my misery and lifting me out of this sea of pain.

Although God never literally rescued me, the Lord used other people to save me from drowning, both physically and emotionally.

For example, on a trip to Hawaii the Lord sent a total stranger to deliver me from the merciless power of the ocean's tide. Always ready for a new adventure, Ken and I decided to visit Hanama Bay. Our friends had told us about a blow-hole in the reef, a little way from the main beach, so we began hiking along the shoreline. We had heard that the islanders called this hole "the toilet bowl" because the ocean washed into the reef with such force that the water would rise and drop several feet in a few seconds.

Rounding a bend, I saw several young guys already in the "bowl." Without a second thought, I jumped in. From that point on, I was tossed like a rag doll, total-ly at the mercy of the mighty current. Each time my head broke through the water's surface, I would gasp for air before being grabbed by the tide and dragged under water. I helplessly, watched my life pass before my eyes as I slipped further and fur-ther underneath the reef and closer to being pulled out to sea. Just when I thought that my lungs would burst from the lack of oxygen, a strong wave hurled me up to the top, and someone grasped my arm, pulling me to safety. Relief flooded over me as I stood shaking from the fear of such a close call. Realizing the danger that I had been in, I thanked God for saving me through the kind act of a total stranger.

This memory gives me hope as I struggle to keep my head above the waters of grief that threaten to overwhelm me. Just as I feel like I'm going under, the phone rings. It is a church member, wanting to know if she can pray with me. She has heard about my miscarriage, and after experiencing three of her own, she needed to call and share my sorrow. Once again, just in the nick of time, God reaches out to me through the voice of a sympathetic friend, rescuing me from drowning in the depths of my depression.

Lord, when I am sinking in the darkness of despair, deliver me with the light of your presence. Only by grasping your lifeline of salvation will my soul find safety. Please rescue me with the almighty power of your everlasting arms.

Light in the Darkness

God is light and in him there is no darkness at all.
1 John 1:5 (NRSV)

After my second miscarriage, I seemed to slip into a black hole where no light could survive. Depression was a daily battle, and I knew that I was losing the war. Sometimes I was sure that I couldn't cry another tear, and still more would come. Other times I longed for tears to wash away the terrible aching inside, and none appeared. I was just so tired of fighting the pain. I wanted to crawl into a cave and hide from all of the memories of the past few days. Maybe then I could find some rest.

I wished I was more like the little girl who often walked home with her father late in the evening across the moonless prairie. When a friend asked her if she were afraid of the dark, she shook her head and replied, "My father knows the way. As long as I keep my hand in his, I don't need to see where I'm going."

Lord, you know the darkness of my heart. I'm giving you my tears of disappointment. I pray for the faith of this little girl. Even though I can't fully understand the way that you are leading me, I know I'm headed home, and that's all that really matters. I thank you for holding tightly to my hand until I can once again see your light in my life.

Face-to-face

...You, O LORD, are in the midst of this people; for you, O LORD, are seen face to face.

Numbers 14:14 (NRSV)

When I was ten years old, I began writing to a girl from Singapore. Since then we have been pen pals and close friends. I have often imagined traveling to the Orient to meet my pen pal, and seeing in person all the exotic places that she had described. What fun we would have together touring her country! In fact, just being able to meet her face-to-face would be a dream come true.

I guess I feel the same way about God, especially since my miscarriage. I've read the letters in the Bible, and I long for heaven, where earth's sorrows are no more. But most of all, I want to talk to the Lord face-to-face, just like I would with a close friend.

Even as a small child this desire burned brightly in my heart. I used to go to church and pretend that God sat in front of the octagon stained-glass window that was in the center of the sanctuary. Around noon, the sun would cast rays of light through the glass, making rainbows in the pews. I could almost picture God's smile in the sunbeam, and a soft glow would fill me as I sang the closing song.

I guess that's why I long for the day when I will be able to see the face of the Lord and personally talk to God about all the questions in my heart. I know then that the Lord will explain the reasons for my tragedies. I just pray that God will give me enough strength to hang on until then.

Lord, although I can't see you face-to-face, I know that your arms ache to shelter me from this overwhelming sadness of my soul. My greatest need is to catch a glimpse of your presence as I struggle to survive the calamity at hand.

Burdens and Blame

Cast your burden on the Lord, and he will sustain you; he will never permit the righteous to be moved.

Psalm 55:22 (NRSV)

For some reason I have a tendency to pretend that I'm Wonder Woman, capable of carrying all of life's problems single-handedly on my shoulders. When my burdens become so heavy that I can no longer hide the fact that I'm only five foot two inches tall, and rather puny, I often unload them on my husband's tired back and blame him for my troubles. Casting blame, I've found, is much easier than casting burdens.

During the first few days that followed my miscarriage, I kept most of my grief inside and preferred to be alone. My body seemed to go into a protective state of shock, and it was easy to deny the terrible effects of the tragedy. As time passed, however, this numbness began to wear off. I was suddenly hit anew with the awful reality that my baby was gone.

Anger at the unfairness of my child's untimely death came boiling to the surface and, in frustration, I lashed out at God and everyone else. Often those closest to me suffered the most. My husband, Ken, could do nothing right; everything he did irritated me. Either he was too busy to listen or he'd sit in silence while I opened up my heart to him.

What I didn't understand at the time was that husbands and wives tend to react differently to grief. Ken's means of coping with our child's death was to bury himself in work and forget the heartaches of the past by concentrating on the future. I thought that his withdrawal from me meant that he didn't really care about my feelings. This resulted only in more pain.

Even though I should have cast my burdens on God, I piled them on my husband instead. Rather than suffocating Ken with my sorrow, I ought to have shared it with my pastor or a trained Christian counselor. Perhaps then I wouldn't have had to pretend that I was Wonder Woman or blame someone else for my inadequacy.

Lord, although I've blamed others for my deficiencies, from this day forward I want your help in casting my burdens on you. Only by relying on your guidance and the godly wisdom of pastors and counselors can I find power enough to persevere.

Bottled-up Grief

A voice was heard in Ramah of painful crying and deep sadness: Rachel crying for her children. She refused to be comforted, because her children are dead! But this is what the LORD *says: "Stop crying; don't let your eyes fill with tears. You will be rewarded for your work!" says the* LORD. *"So there is hope for you in the future," says the* LORD. *"Your children will return."*

Jeremiah 31:15–16 (NCV)

One decision I regretted after my second miscarriage was suppressing my grief inside of me instead of sharing it with family and friends. Since few knew of my tragedy, I received little support. No cards, no gifts, no words of encouragement. Nothing like I had experienced during my first loss. Although my heart longed for the comfort of human companionship, I was too embarrassed to admit that my worst nightmare had happened again.

Maybe the timing of my loss was another reason why I was hesitant to tell others about my tragedy. Since I was only six weeks into my pregnancy, the death of my second child was much easier to hide—no maternity clothes, no weight gain to speak of, no telltale signs that were reminders of what might have been. It seemed rather pointless to tell people about my miscarriage when they hadn't known I was expecting.

As a result of keeping my grief tethered inside, I suffered silently and all alone, totally isolated from the loving support that my soul so desperately craved. If only I had someone to pray with me, someone to hold my hand and cry with me, I wouldn't feel such abandonment in my time of need. I continued desperately treading water, waiting for someone to rescue me from the relentless waves of despair.

Finally, after exhausting all of my self-determination, I turned to the only two sources of strength that had faithfully stood by me throughout the storms of the past—God and my husband. I could feel the Lord's love in my husband's gentle touch, and I thanked God for giving me a companion who was slowly becoming my soul mate. Even though he sometimes struggled in his attempts to comfort me, he never gave up. And that was one quality I admired and adored. Fortunately, I was not the lone survivor of shipwrecked dreams. My husband and I could face the future, knowing that God was at the helm of our lives.

Lord, I thank you for providing me with such a devoted lifelong companion. Even though the loss of a second child overwhelms our hearts with sorrow, I know that you will guide us through this ocean of grief together.

Headed the Right Direction

I will seek the lost, and I will bring back the strayed, and I will bind up the injured, and I will strengthen the weak.

Ezekiel 34:16 (NRSV)

As time passed after my second miscarriage, I often wondered about the direction I was headed in my life. Was I following the Lord's will? On such days I would pull out my Bible and flip through the pages, noting all the verses that I had underlined in red. Sometimes I would find a dated event written next to a text, reminding me of its personal value during a specific trial. These notations of how the Lord had led me in the past gave me encouragement for the present.

For example, whenever I was tempted to believe that God had left me hopelessly lost in a mountain of grief, I would remember the hike that my mother and I had taken in Colorado. Late one summer afternoon we started down a mountain path, stopping every few minutes to take pictures and chat. Red ribbons marked the trail, and we simply hiked from tree to tree, fascinated by the squirrels and the beautiful scenery. Suddenly, a slight chill ran down my back as I saw shadows beginning to emerge in the forest. Glancing at my watch, I noticed how quickly the hours had passed and how far we had yet to go.

About that time we reached a muddy clearing, and on the other side no red markers were in sight. With darkness only minutes away, my mother and I searched frantically. Just then, two dogs and two men appeared, jogging up the mountain toward us. At the time, I never stopped to ponder how odd it was for these elderly men to be running up a mountain at sunset. I asked if they knew how to find the path that we had been following. They informed us that we were on an abandoned trail that had not been maintained for years, but if we would go back across the clearing, we would find a red marker hidden behind a big rock. From there, we would see the others. Before we could thank them, they disappeared behind a bend. We soon found the missing red marker and followed the path to the village below without any further problems.

Just as the Lord sent help when I was lost in the mountains of Colorado, so God offers loving guidance by giving me special verses in the Bible to keep my steps headed for my heavenly home. Even when the darkness of my grief shadows my way, I can rely on scripture to be a "lamp to my feet and a light to my path" (Psalm 119:105, NRSV). Despite tragic setbacks, with the Lord in the lead, I know that I am bound to reach my destination.

For direction in life, check the map of God's word.

Finding Rest in Release

Come to me, all you that are weary and are carrying heavy burdens, and I will give you rest. Take my yoke upon you, and learn from me; for I am gentle and humble in heart, and you will find rest for your souls.

Matthew 11:28–29 (NRSV)

Sleep and rest must have two different definitions because although I slept after my miscarriage, a long time passed before I found any true rest. At first I felt like I was living in a nightmare and that at any time I would wake up from it and be pregnant with a healthy baby. But as days passed, the reality of my loss slowly sunk in, and I longed to escape the aching of my soul through a good night's sleep. So often, however, I would lay in bed at night with my mind set on replay and my body unable to press the "off" button. Even when sleep finally came, I often felt as tired in the morning as I had the night before. I can remember wishing that dawn would never come. Then the heartaches of the past wouldn't slap me in the face with cold memories each time I opened my eyes. More than the physical sleep, I desperately needed emotional rest to soothe my restless spirit.

During one sleepless night, I stumbled to my living room and pulled my Bible out from underneath the coffee table. Although the words seemed jumbled together like a giant jigsaw puzzle, I was determined to sort out some kind of meaning. Even when I grew tired of reading and the stories seemed outdated and inapplicable, I pressed on, hoping to bring some order to my mixed-up life. I wasn't surprised when I read that Jesus promised me rest. I guess the surprise came when he actually did it. How he woke me from my living nightmare, I'll never know. Was it just time? Or was it surrender?

Perhaps I was much like the little girl who wanted her doll mended, but wouldn't let her mother take it from her arms. At last, the mother in exasperation exclaimed, "How can I fix it for you, dear, if you won't let me have it?" Maybe I was hanging on so tightly to my pain that God couldn't pry it out of my heart until I was willing to let go.

Lord, you see the sorrow buried deep in my soul. I want to surrender it all to you. Help me rest on the promise of your name—my Prince of Peace.

The Power of a Name

But now thus says the LORD... "Do not fear, for I have redeemed you; I have called you by name, you are mine."

Isaiah 43:1 (NRSV)

Meanings of names have always fascinated me. During my second pregnancy I decided to look up the definition of my own and discovered that Melissa meant "honeybee." I sincerely hope that my parents chose this name because they thought I was sweet and not because I could sting. Whatever the reason, all my life I have gone by this one name, and it has become a part of my identity.

Although I spent hours trying to decide what I would call my baby when it was born, I never followed through with this desire when I miscarried. Now I wish I had. Somehow I believe that having a name associated with my loss would have brought me more comfort. Perhaps then society might have recognized the enormity of my grief. A genetic mistake or a cruel twist of fate hadn't just occurred. It was a real child, with flesh and blood, who died the day I miscarried. Yet no one came to a funeral. No one brought casseroles. No one sent flowers. Deep in my heart I was tempted to believe that no one really cared. No one but me.

One of my best friends defied society's silence about miscarriage by mailing memorial cards to all of her family and friends that included the name of her child, the date of its death, and a Bible text of assurance. When I received mine, tears trickled down my cheeks, not only for her loss but also from the ardent desire to make my baby's death real in the world's eyes and not just in my own. I was especially touched by the name she had chosen, Destiny Joy. She explained in the card that this child was destined to bring her joy in Heaven. What a witness of her faith and trust in God.

I admire my friend's wisdom in naming her child because I believe it helped bring about closure, which is an important part of the healing process. I'm also thankful that according to God's promise, I, too, will someday know my child's name, and no one will ever forget it.

Lord, it saddens me that this world does little to comfort parents mourning a miscarried baby and even less to commemorate its death. By the power of your name, please give me the courage to reverse society's failures and turn them into public demonstrations of your unfailing love.

Mirrored Mistakes

The cords of death entangled me, the anguish of the grave came upon me; I was overcome by trouble and sorrow. Then I called on the name of the LORD: "O LORD, save me!" ...Be at rest once more, O my soul, for the LORD has been good to you. For you, O LORD, have delivered my soul from death, my eyes from tears, my feet from stumbling, that I may walk before the LORD in the land of the living.

Psalm 116:3–4,7–9 (NIV)

Little things often brought back a tidal wave of emotion as time passed after my miscarriage. Watching a television commercial advertising diapers or seeing a billboard sporting a newborn's grin could easily reduce me to tears. Although most of my family and friends thought that I had recovered, my heart still lay broken inside, and sorrow threatened to overflow at any minute.

One day, for instance, I simply opened my mail and found a sympathy card along with a birth announcement from my pen pal in Singapore. The combination of the two instantly brought back biting pain, and I honestly wondered if I'd ever find true healing.

Another time my emotions threatened to overflow was when I was at the mall with a friend. Shopping seemed like a great means of escape and, for once, I was certain that I would enjoy myself. This girlfriend didn't have any children, so I felt safe—no baby strollers, no diaper changes, no memories. As I happily browsed through some sale items, a voice suddenly called to me from behind a clothes rack. As my girlfriend came into sight, she held up a tiny pink dress, full of ruffles and lace. Instantly, I felt my cheeks growing hot as she bubbled, "Don't you think this is just perfect for a baby gift! I think I'll get it for one of the new mothers at church." I nodded my head, unable to speak, and quickly pretended to be absorbed in my shopping. I felt like a knife had just been thrust into my heart. Somehow the rest of the shopping spree lost its appeal. I simply wanted to go home. How could my friend be so thoughtless?

As this thought echoed in my mind, I remembered my reaction to my neighbor's miscarriage, which occurred before I had had my own. She hadn't been pregnant long before she lost her baby. I had celebrated Christmas with her and could remember when she received a pair of maternity pants. We had both laughed at how big they seemed. Then, a few days later she mentioned that she wasn't pregnant any longer. I never thought anymore about it—no card, no flowers, not even an "I'm sorry." I simply ignored her pain. How could I have been so uncaring?

Lord, no one is perfect. We all make mistakes. Help me to be more aware of others' pain, especially now that I have suffered my own. As I pour out my heart to you in prayer, forgive me for my past blindness, and open my eyes to the present needs of those suffering around me.

From Grumbling to Gratitude

So I tell you, whatever you ask for in prayer, believe that you have received it, and it will be yours.

Mark 11:24 (NRSV)

A s the weeks slipped by, I longed for more emotional support. Because my husband and I had decided to keep our last pregnancy a secret until the end of the first trimester, few knew about my miscarriage. Although we had attended our church for two years, I didn't feel close enough to any of the members to say, "Please pray for me. I just lost my second child." I found myself resenting the fact that no one knew about my pain, even though I was too uncomfortable to tell anyone about it.

During my morning worship one day, I began talking to God about how lonely I felt. In desperation I had asked my neighbor across the street to have her church pray for me because I felt so isolated. I began wondering why I hadn't made closer friendships among my own church family. *Maybe I should go to a different church. Perhaps mine just isn't friendly enough.* In my anger, I doubted if they would even miss me. As I continued my study, negative thoughts persisted. Suddenly, the Lord seemed to whisper, "Perhaps you should do something about your loneliness instead of just complaining about your church."

Shocked at the simplicity of God's solution to my troubles, I began considering ways that I could get better acquainted with the women of my church. The idea of starting a women's prayer group in my home popped into my mind. Why, of course! Why hadn't I thought of this before? Immediately, I began writing down a list of people to invite for supper and a short Bible study. Surely, there had to be other lonely women that needed friends like me. Dialing the phone, my fingers trembled as I timidly invited my first guest. To my delight, she gratefully accepted, as did eight others.

The night of the supper quickly arrived, and all too soon, it was time to tell the guests my intentions. To my utter amazement, they whole-heartedly welcomed the idea of starting a prayer group, and many shared testimonies of the struggles that they were facing in their lives. Although not all could relate to the loss of a child, everyone had experienced some sort of pain, and many even shed tears. My heart glowed with the warmth of friendship as we finished the Bible study with a word of prayer and hugged each other good-bye. How could I ever have thought that my church family was cold or uncaring? Grateful that God had interrupted my self-pity with such a wonderful idea, I bowed my head and prayed,

Thank you, Lord, for not giving up on me, even when I am tempted to believe that no one cares. Most of all, I praise you for introducing these precious women to me and making them truly my friends.

Finding The Right Words

The LORD has sent me to comfort those who mourn... He sent me to give them flowers in place of their sorrow, olive oil in place of tears, and joyous praise in place of broken hearts.

Isaiah 61:2–3 (CEV)

Picking up the phone, I could hear the emotional strain in my friend's voice. Instantly, I knew that something was terribly wrong.

"I... uh... I just lost my baby."

As sobs punctuated each syllable, my heart went out to her. Memories of my own miscarriages rushed back into my mind. Listening to the details of her story, I desperately searched for the best way to ease her sorrow, but no ideas came. One would think that after two miscarriages, I would be able to come up with some words of wisdom, but none seemed to accurately express the deep empathy I felt for her. I didn't dare use the standard pat phrases, because I knew from experience that they brought little or no comfort. Instead, I found myself saying very little. In fact, the more I listened and the less I said, the better off we both were.

As we finished talking and crying together, we prayed over the phone. I can't remember what words I used, but they must have had some impact because afterward her voice sounded more at ease. Promising to call in a few days, I hung up the phone and let out a deep sigh. Relief flooded over me as I bowed my head and prayed:

Lord, even though I understand a little of what my friend is going through, I still need your wisdom to know how to touch others with your love. Please send your Spirit to speak through me when I have no words to say. Make me willing to listen to other's heartaches and take the time to weep with them. Only then will I be able to share the comfort you've given to me in my life.

Tears of Empathy

Jesus wept.
        John 11:35 (NKJV)

Such powerful words! Although I have heard that this verse is the shortest in the Bible, its significance far outweighs its length. Why would Jesus bother to cry over the death of Lazarus when he had the power to restore his life? He could have smiled in anticipation of his friend's resurrection from the grave, but instead tears streamed down his cheeks and his shoulders shook from the uncontrollable sobs of a broken heart. Why did he grieve over this temporary loss of one of his closest friends? Perhaps the answer to this question lies in a story I once heard about a little girl who was late getting home from school.

When Carrie walked through the front door, her mother impatiently asked her where she had been. The small girl quietly answered, "I was with my friend. She was crying because her doll's head fell off."

"So did you help her put the doll's head back on?" her mother inquired.

"No, we couldn't fix it," Carrie said sadly.

"Then why, dear, are you so late getting home?" Mother pressed, a bit irritated at her daughter's tardiness.

With a tiny tremble of her bottom lip, the little girl simply replied, "I decided to stay with my friend and just help her cry."

Lord, I want to empathize with those hurting around me like you did when you were here on this earth. Help me to speak your words of love and be a faithful friend. Thank you for the privilege of being your hands that can wipe away others' tears.

The Grief of Grandparents

But the LORD's love for those who respect him continues forever and ever, and his goodness continues to their grandchildren.

Psalm 103:17 (NCV)

Losing a baby can have a dramatic effect on others besides just the parents. Grandparents, for example, often grieve intensely after a miscarriage, especially if the extended family has been excited about the pregnancy from the beginning.

At church one day a visiting pastor approached me. As I reached out to shake his hand, I was surprised to see tears glistening in his eyes. Although he was better acquainted with my parents, he had heard about my miscarriages and felt comfortable confiding in me. With a slight quiver in his voice, he whispered, "My daughter just lost her baby. She was two months along, and it was our first grandchild. I just had to tell you. I knew you would understand." I nodded my head and squeezed his hand.

Memories of a family Christmas gathering flashed through my mind. I had discovered that I was pregnant soon after Thanksgiving and had purposely waited until Christmas to surprise my parents with the news. Carefully, I had constructed a card, written from the baby's point-of-view. It said: "A precious bundle will arrive next September." I knew that they would be thrilled. I had tried for so long to get pregnant, I think they had almost given up hope of ever having grandchildren. I waited excitedly until all the presents were unwrapped and then, with a twinkle in my eye, I handed my parents the card. When they realized that their grandbaby was on the way, my mother burst into tears and joyfully ran to hug me. Even my dad's eyes misted over as he joined our embrace. My grandmothers and great-grandmother also rejoiced, making it one of the happiest Christmases ever. No one could wait for the little one's arrival.

Then, only a month later, I miscarried. The news was devastating for the entire family. The eager anticipation vanished, and a terrible sorrow took its place.

Now that I look back, it is much easier for me to grasp the significance of the pain in my parents' eyes. They, too, had to struggle along the long road of healing, while trying at the same time to support their children. Sometimes it's not easy being a grandparent, especially when that chance is taken away unexpectedly.

Grandparents and God have a lot in common. They both love their children more than others think possible.

Blessings in Disguise

For I am convinced that neither death, nor life, nor angels, nor rulers, nor things present, nor things to come, nor powers, nor height, nor depth, nor anything else in all creation, will be able to separate us from the love of God in Christ Jesus our Lord.

Romans 8:38–39 (NRSV)

I would like for you to consider giving grief recovery classes for the benefit of the community, as well as for our own church family." The pastor's words came as a total surprise. Although I had spent considerable time researching and writing about miscarriages during the previous few years, I still felt unqualified for such an involved ministry. Yet the opportunity of helping others work through their grief truly interested me, since I had personally experienced its devastating effects after the loss of my own children.

As I hesitated a moment before responding to the pastor's suggestion, I suddenly realized that I was not the same person I had been a few years ago. In the past I would have shrunk from the fear of speaking in front of an audience, but the desire to comfort those suffering from a pain similar to mine gave me courage that I had never before known. Perhaps God was leading me into this ministry in order to bring further fulfillment in my own life, as well as to help others in need.

Another change that I couldn't help but notice as I looked back over my life was the growth of my marriage. By weathering the fierce storms of tragedy, Ken and I had learned how to support each other and our relationship had improved. When trials surfaced in the future, we would be better prepared to meet them.

My relationship with God was also stronger since the loss of my children. It seemed that I had only two choices in the face of death—either trust the Lord or forsake him completely. Although the battle of indecision had been fierce, I was thankful for the peace that I had found in my decision to follow Christ at all costs. Only through God could I find the hope of being reunited with my children someday in heaven. What comfort this promise had brought me throughout the previous years.

Suddenly I realized that the pastor was still waiting for an answer. Mustering up my courage, I bravely said, "Please pray with me about leading the grief seminar, and if that's what God wants me to do, then I am certainly willing."

Lord, we've been through so much together and, as a result, I've grown in so many different ways. I can't say that I would want to do it all over, but even if that happened, I know that nothing could separate me from your love.

God's Honor Roll

Those who war against you shall be as nothing at all. For I, the LORD your God, hold your right hand; it is I who say to you, "Do not fear, I will help you."

Isaiah 41:12–13 (NRSV)

The other day, when I was cleaning out my closet, I discovered a box that I had packed away shortly after my miscarriage. Gently lifting its cover, my eyes rested on a beautifully woven baby afghan. I lovingly ran my fingers over the soft white yarn. Memories of the day I'd received this special gift floated back into my mind, and a smile played gently on my lips. I had been pregnant then, full of so many plans for the perfect nursery. A former teacher that I had grown to love like one of my own grandmothers heard the happy news and had knitted the afghan for me. I knew that each stitch had been carefully sewn with love, and her thoughtfulness meant so much to me.

Then the day came when I had to call and tell her that I had lost my baby. I could almost see the tears in her eyes as we grieved together on the phone. A few days later, I opened the mailbox to find a second package from her. In it I discovered a note and a tape. With wisdom gained only from years of heartache, this precious friend poured out her love to me in a letter.

I will never forget the impact of her words. She gently reminded me that God offers love in abundance, even during the fiercest trials. The Lord never forsakes any of his children, no matter what heartaches come their way. Even amidst the battles of life, God is a refuge, restoring strength to the weak, comfort to the afflicted, and hope to the hopeless. As the Lord's healing mends broken hearts, so God's people are given the freedom to share their triumphs with others that are struggling, waiting for the day when sorrows will be no more.

She ended her letter by encouraging me to remain faithful to the Lord at all costs. Then my life would be a living testimony of the power of restoration, making me a special part of God's "honor roll."

As I slowly put the lid back on the afghan's box, I prayed,

Lord, help me to persevere even when I don't have enough strength left to fight on my own. Although my heart is wounded, I long to stay true to you. Give me the victory over self-reliance and the fortitude of your peace.

The Peace of Surrender

Peace I leave with you; my peace I give to you. I do not give to you as the world gives. Do not let your heart be troubled, and do not let them be afraid.

John 14:27 (NRSV)

Lord, when will you give me a child? I was tired of waiting and tired of trusting. How could I go on this way?

Opening my Bible, I stumbled across the story of Hannah asking the same question. She found herself childless in a time when a woman's worth was measured by her fertility. In her desperation for a son, she vowed to give him to God all the days of his life. I never really wondered why the Lord did not grant her request sooner, but suddenly the answer seemed crystal clear. Her prayer was answered only when she was willing to give the desires of her heart completely over to God.

Startled, I contemplated the impact of this revelation on my life. Could God be waiting on me? Throughout the years, I had often tried to second-guess the Lord's will. Surely the plans that I had made for my life were in harmony with God's! Never once had I considered a life without children.

Lord, are you asking me to surrender totally my longing for a baby to your will— even if it means never having children of my own?

As my mind whirled in confusion, my heart already knew the answer. God was not asking anything more of me than what the Lord had already given. Even if I never got pregnant again, my heart's desires could still be fulfilled in a thousand different ways. I just had to trust in the one who had given up everything for me.

With tears in my eyes, I whispered, "All right, Lord, whatever you want is what I want for my future." Although I thought I'd be crushed under the enormity of such a sacrifice, my heart was filled instead with peace—the kind the world and I won't ever fully understand.

Surrender is the key that unlocks God's freedom.

Cradled in Comfort

This is what the LORD says: "I will give her peace that will flow to her like a river... Like babies you will be nursed and held in my arms and bounced on my knees. I will comfort you as a mother comforts her child..."

Isaiah 66:12–13 (NCV)

After losing two children, I never thought I could hold a baby again and feel anything but heart-wrenching pain, but today was different. It was a simple encounter. I ran into a friend changing her little girl in the restroom. I immediately felt trapped. I couldn't just walk by without speaking to her, and yet a lump caught in my throat as I stared into her baby's dark eyes. *She's perfect,* I thought. *So delicate and beautiful. The same age my little one would have been if...* Instantly, tears threatened to spill down my cheeks as I silently pleaded, *Lord, I need to feel your peace.*

Surprised by the swiftness of God's answer to my cry, I could feel the pain of the past soften. I watched in wonder as the little girl closed her long, dark eyelashes. Perhaps the strange look on my face gave my friend the courage to ask if I would like to hold her precious little bundle. Hesitating a moment, I reached out and gently took the sleepy infant into my arms. Suddenly, a picture of Jesus holding me tightly flashed through my mind. I couldn't help but smile, for deep in my heart I heard a tender voice whisper:

Rest now, my child. You'll always find the comfort you need here in the cradle of my arms.

In the Arms of the Good Shepherd

He takes care of his people like a shepherd. He gathers them like lambs in his arms and carries them close to him.

Isaiah 40:11 (NCV)

One of my favorite pictures is Jesus hugging a little lamb. Perhaps this portrait is special because I always imagined that he was holding me. I liked the shepherd imagery so much that when I got pregnant I decided to decorate my nursery with lambs, using this picture as a centerpiece. I bought wallpaper, stuffed animals, and blankets, all with this theme in mind. Then I lost my baby, and for some time the sight of lambs brought tears instead of joy. During this time, I felt lost in a storm of circumstances. Where was the Good Shepherd? Why did I feel so alone? Desperately, I yearned for a haven of rest from my turbulent emotions. The desire of being close to the Lord continued to deepen and, as time passed, I found the comfort that my soul needed.

Years later, at my grandmother's funeral, I stumbled across a tombstone engraved with a little lamb, and as I read the words, "Our Baby," tears trickled down my cheeks. Memories of the shepherd picture flashed back into my mind. Suddenly I realized that Jesus had held me both during my tragedy and through my grieving, even when I couldn't feel his arms. He had never let me go! Although the pain still lingered in my heart and God's, I knew that I could always curl up in the Lord's lap and let the Good Shepherd bind up my wounds. Somehow, just knowing that I was safe in God's fold gave me hope and comfort for the future.

Lord, like a little lamb, I need your constant care. Keep me wrapped inside your arms of love as you restore my soul with your gentle touch.

The Strength of Companionship

Surely he [Jesus] has borne our griefs and carried our sorrows.
Isaiah 53:4 (NKJV)

Being carried in loving arms warms the soul kind of like a cup of hot chocolate on a cold, winter night. At least that's how I felt on my wedding day when my husband carried me over the threshold. In his arms I was ready to face the future, confident and unafraid.

Although time has a way of tarnishing such high expectations, I have to admit that my husband has grown more supportive of me throughout the years. For example, after our second miscarriage he carried more than his share of the household duties, giving me the time I needed to recover from the shock of such a devastating tragedy. He was careful not to demand too much from me, and he even tried to make extra time to listen as I shared my feelings. His support often lifted my spirits and set my mind on more positive thoughts. Even amidst the pain, he had learned constructive ways of bearing the weight of our grief. As I admire my husband's inner strength, I am reminded that God is always ready to give his children the emotional and physical power they need to meet the challenges of the day.

One memory in particular brings this truth home to my heart. It was a beautiful tropical afternoon when Ken, my mother, and I decided to hike down a steep incline to see one of Guam's many spectacular waterfalls. At the time, my husband and I were serving a two-year mission call to this small Pacific island, and Mom had decided to spend a few weeks sightseeing with us. The trail down the hill was steep and uneven. Just as the waterfall was coming into sight, mom stumbled and fell into a hidden hole. Moaning in pain, her ankle obviously broken, my mother insisted on crawling, but Ken bravely lifted her onto his back and carried her up the steep incline to the car. Afterward, mom was quite thankful that God had given my husband such physical strength in her time of need.

Memories like this one encourage me as I mourn the loss of our second child. Although exhaustion threatens to overwhelm my soul, the warmth of my husband's arms renews my spirit. Whether I'm lacking in emotional or physical strength, I can find comfort in the strength that God so faithfully supplies through my loving companion.

Lord, I pray that I might be a support to my husband, just as he has been to me. Thank you for carrying my burdens with hands strong enough to form the world, yet gentle enough to wipe the tears from my eyes.

The Apple of God's Eye

Truly one who touches you touches the apple of my eye.
Zechariah 2:8 (NRSV)

Mother's Day. Most women look forward to this day of recognition. For some it will include flowers, restaurants, homemade cards, breakfast in bed, gifts, and much more. However, for someone who has lost a child, Mother's Day can be the worst time of the year. I know. I've tried to forget about this day, but even at church one cannot escape it. Often the sermon on this occasion centers around biblical women who have proven their faithfulness to God by raising godly children. Then a closing song such as "Faith of our Mothers" is usually sung. The pastoral prayer, too, expresses appreciation for the dedication of mothers. Those who are childless often leave the service feeling unappreciated and less than an ideal woman.

This year, however, the women's ministry leaders decided to try something new. Not wanting anyone to be left out, each female in the congregation was given a beautiful velvet bag of bath crystals with a gold card that spoke of the value of women. The pastor's wife explained the gift by saying that all females are "spiritual mothers" of the church, whether they are actual mothers, grand-mothers, young mothers-to-be, or childless mothers that assist others with their children. Every woman plays a vital role in the body of Christ, and all should be recognized for their special ministry. For the first time, I left the service with a song in my heart, praising the Lord for the thoughtfulness of my church family.

Lord, I'm so glad that you love me just the way I am. I don't have to be a mother to know that I am one of your precious children. Thank you for the privilege of being the apple of your eye.

Teardrops in the Rain

But the eyes of the LORD are on those who fear him, on those whose hope is in his unfailing love.

Psalm 33:18 (NIV)

For as long as I can remember, eyes have intrigued me. I have often wondered what God's eyes must look like. Are they blue or brown or maybe green? Do they sparkle in the light and have long, dark eyelashes? One thing I know for sure is that neither God nor I can wait until the day when neither of us will ever have tears in our eyes again, but until then, I know that I will never be out of the Lord's sight.

I was reminded during my visit to the Louvre in Paris of how God continually watches over me. One of the highlights of the tour was seeing the famous painting of Mona Lisa. As I stared at the portrait, her eyes seemed to follow me. Even when I walked to the other side of the room, she appeared to be looking directly at me. The tour guide explained that this phenomenon was the result of a special painting technique that was used by the world's best artists. As the tour continued, I just couldn't stop thinking about the similarities in Mona Lisa's eyes and the Lord's.

I bet that is what the psalmist meant when he said that God's eyes are always upon his children. Even when my vision is blurred with tears, I know my Lord sees my misery. The sorrow of God must be unbearable as the Lord watches all the suffering in the world.

When I was little I used to think that one way God expressed sadness was through raindrops. Perhaps it was appropriate that it was pouring the day the doctor could not find my baby's heartbeat. As I left the clinic with my eyes full of tears, raindrops splashed down all around me, and the darkness of my heart mirrored the stormy weather. Suddenly, a memory broke through my mind like a ray of sunlight piercing a black cloud. I was a youngster again, walking through the mud puddles and thinking that the Lord must be crying really hard to have shed so many teardrops. As I pondered this childish musing, I was reminded that even amidst my pain God's eyes never leave me, and often they are filled with tears, too.

Lord, I thank you for always watching over me, even when I cry. I can't wait for the day when we can wipe away our tears forever, and there will be "no more death, nor sorrow, nor crying… for the former things have passed away."
Revelation 21:4 (NKJV)

A Harvest of Joy

May those who sow in tears reap with shouts of joy. Those who go out weeping, bearing the seed for sowing, shall come home with shouts of joy, carrying their sheaves.

Psalm 126:5–6 (NRSV)

Despite my lack of a green thumb, I have found that sowing tears like sowing seeds can produce a bountiful harvest in more ways than one. Perhaps the secret to this discovery is buried in the transformation of both, performed by the miraculous touch of the master gardener.

Growing up in the city, I never learned to appreciate the fine art of gardening, unlike my husband, who grew up on a farm. All of his life, he couldn't wait to have his own row to hoe. Soon after we got married he hand-dug a garden spot and began planting a variety of vegetables. Not being one to enjoy getting dirty, I was surprised by my astute ability to hand him the seeds. They were so tiny that I had a hard time believing that they would actually amount to anything. But I resolved to be a supportive wife and pretended that I was having fun deciding where each kind of seed should be planted.

Even though I don't have much of a green thumb, I know enough about gardening to deduce that sowing seeds is a picnic compared to sowing tears. Believe me, I speak from experience: I have never cried so much in my life as when I lost my baby. It's hard to imagine that those tears could ever produce joy, but that is exactly what God's word promises. I guess it's kind of like trying to explain how a tiny shriveled-up seed can turn into a luscious red tomato. Both transformations take place through the miraculous touch of the one who gives life "and life more abundantly" (John 10:10).

God can turn a seed of sorrow into a harvest of happiness.

Flying on Wings of Thanksgiving

You have turned my mourning into dancing; you have taken off my sack-cloth and clothed me with joy, so that my soul may praise you and not be silent. O LORD my God, I will give thanks to you forever.

Psalm 30:11–12 (NRSV)

I have often wished that I had wings that would whisk me away from the troubles of this life. Then I would not have to endure the misery of this world, which is so evident all around me. Sometimes, when I am certain that I cannot tolerate the ugliness a moment longer, I am reminded of the patient endurance I one day discovered, masked in the beauty of a monarch butterfly.

With the delight of a child, I watched in silent wonder as the magnificent creature unfolded it velvety wings as it rested on my arm. I couldn't imagine why it had chosen such a spot to sport its simple elegance, but I certainly didn't mind. Marveling at its intricate design, I was sure that no human work of art could ever compare. Then suddenly a puff of wind caught its wings and the butterfly took flight, dancing before my eyes as gracefully as a ballerina.

Watching the monarch float into the distance, I wondered how this small creature could ever survive the harshness of life. Its delicate splendor stood in sharp contrast to the polluted city in which it lived. How did it find such strength in fragility, such majesty in the mundane?

Beholding its beauty, I discovered fresh hope for my heart that I might also soar on wings of thanksgiving through this marred earth. Clothed in the Lord's comfort, I could sing a song of gladness and praise the God of joy. Like the carefree butterfly, I could rest in God's promise of refuge, thanking the Lord for peace amidst the clamor of life.

Lord, like a caterpillar is transformed into a magnificent butterfly, so you can turn my trials into hidden blessings of joy. I want to thank you for renewing my spirit with the delicate beauty of your love.

God's Special Treasure

I bore you on eagles' wings and brought you to myself. Now therefore, if you indeed obey my voice and keep my covenant, then you shall be a special treasure to me above all people.

Exodus 19:4–5 (NKJV)

Does God really care about me personally? Does the Lord of the universe have the time to save a grieving mother from a storm of sorrow caused by a miscarriage? I've often wondered about these questions, and discovering the answers has made a tremendous impact on my life.

One of the first times that I pondered the Lord's personal involvement in the world was on a memorable ride in an airplane. As I gazed down at the earth, skyscrapers were as small as candy bars, and automobiles resembled ants. From my vantage point, I could barely make out the forms of what must have been people scurrying down the streets. I certainly couldn't see their faces. The heavens seemed to swallow them in the distance. I wondered how God must view my world from above. Could it be as insignificant as it appeared?

I didn't have time to come to any conclusions because just then the airplane hit turbulence. Grabbing hold of the armrests, I struggled to refasten my seatbelt as the captain's warning thundered over the speaker. The wind buffeted the plane with such force that I was afraid that my cry for help would be lost in its roar. As a knot of fear churned in my stomach, I desperately prayed to God to save me. Although I had always wanted to soar through the skies like an eagle, at that moment I would have been quite happy with the monotonous life of an ostrich, as long as my feet were planted on solid ground. Unfortunately, I had little choice but to watch helplessly as the earth grew closer.

The instant the wheels safely touched down, a sigh escaped from the passengers. Never before had I been so thankful for God's immediate response to my prayer. I believe that the Lord must have been listening to my inquiries and decided to show me a vivid display of his personal involvement in my life.

Reflecting back on this experience, I am comforted by the thought that the Lord hears my desperate cry, even during the fiercest storms of tragedy. Although the winds of grief knock me to the ground, my soul continues to fly safely on God's wings of love. I can trust in the Lord's guidance of my life, knowing that he cherishes each of us individually.

Lord, I just want to thank you for caring about a tiny, insignificant life like mine—so much that you would be willing to risk all of heaven to save me. How blessed am I to be called your "special treasure"!

Recording God's Answers to Prayer

The LORD is just in all his ways, and kind in all his doings. The LORD is near to all who call on him... He fulfills the desire of all who fear him; he also hears their cry, and saves them.

Psalm 145:17–19 (NRSV)

Praying for a child can be long and tiring, especially when one doesn't see any immediate results. My husband and I spent more than two years begging God for a baby before I became pregnant the first time. During those years my faith often wavered, and I wondered if the Lord would ever fulfill the desires of my heart.

In the days before my first pregnancy, I discovered that journaling was an effective way of relinquishing my self-control and allowing God's timing to work in my life. By recording my thoughts and feelings on paper, I saw God's answers to my prayers materializing before my eyes. For example, when I began taking fertility drugs I started ovulating regularly. This small success was the first step in the process of discovering that I was producing eggs, and that pregnancy was still possible. Such positive signs bolstered my faith and gave me the needed strength to face the uncertainty of the future.

Finally, after years of waiting, God answered our prayers for a child and I became pregnant, only to lose the baby a few months later. Once again, journaling became my lifesaver. I poured out my anger and frustration to God on paper, and again the Lord rebuilt my trust by showing me evidence of his love through the answers to my prayers.

One technique that proved to be especially helpful in my life I found in Philippians 4:6–7. These verses stress the importance of presenting our requests to God with thanksgiving and, in return, receiving the Lord's peace. Convinced that I should try this approach, I wrote out a prayer of thanksgiving to God. Even though I was not yet pregnant, I praised the Lord for answering my prayer for a baby. Amazingly, the very next month, I discovered that I was again pregnant. Although I lost this child too, God continued to supply tangible answers to my prayers. By recording those responses in writing, I was able to hang on to my faith in the Lord, even when I couldn't understand his leading. No matter what the future holds for me when it comes to having children, I know that the Lord loves me and longs for my eternal happiness. The evidence is all spelled out— right there in my prayer journal.

Lord, thank you for your faithfulness in answering my every prayer.

The Anniversary

The grass withers, the flower fades; but the work of our God will stand forever.

Isaiah 40:8 (NRSV)

As I flipped to the next month on the calendar, my eyes immediately focused on the three words boldly written in red, located near the bottom of the page: "Baby's due date." I had forgotten that I had penciled them there.

A sudden burst of emotion rushed through my heart, leaving a lump the size of a grapefruit stuck in my throat. My lips started to tremble, and tears poured down my cheeks. Painful memories flashed vividly into my mind. Each thought battered my heart as I mourned the loss of my little one.

Slumping into a chair, I buried my head in my arms and sobbed uncontrollably. Slowly the minutes ticked by, as sorrow drained from my soul. How could a few simple words bring back such a tidal wave of emotion? I wondered if I had truly found healing, because memories of my miscarriage still hurt so badly. Just then one of my favorite verses came to mind: "Cast all your anxiety upon him, because he cares for you" (1 Peter 5:7, NRSV). Did God care about the suffering caused by the memory of my baby's due date? Was the Lord mourning the loss of a child, too? Pondering the answers to these questions, I felt God's presence strengthening my weary heart. Looking back at my life, I began to realize that healing was a journey filled with many setbacks along the way. With each step, however, the road gets easier, and steady progress is made. As the meaning of this revelation sunk into my mind, renewed courage swelled in my soul.

Then a knock at the door interrupted my thoughts, and my husband walked in carrying a small bouquet of flowers. "Thought you might need a bit of encouragement," he gently explained. Taking the flowers from his hands, I bravely wiped the tears from my eyes and smiled.

He hadn't forgotten, and neither had God. My husband's small act of kindness was a beautiful reminder of God's compassion promised to me in his word. The Lord did care, and as I faced the anniversary of my baby's due date, I knew that God would continue to grant me enough strength for each step along the rugged road to healing.

Lord, although progress can sometimes be slow, please grant me the perseverance to press forward. I know that you are making me whole, and I thank you for giving me your word that someday anniversaries of sorrow will be erased forever by your love.